Play It!

LEVEL 1

A Superfast Way to Learn Awesome Songs
on Your Piano or Keyboard

JAZZ AND FOLK SONGS

By Jennifer Kemmeter and Antimo Marrone

GRAPHIC ARTS
BOOKS®

Library of Congress Control Number: 2021950169

ISBN: 9781513128788 (paperback) | 9781513128795 (hardbound) | 9781513128801 (e-book)

Published by Graphic Arts Books
an imprint of West Margin Press

WEST MARGIN PRESS

WestMarginPress.com

Proudly distributed by Ingram Publisher Services

WEST MARGIN PRESS
Publishing Director: Jennifer Newens
Marketing Manager: Alice Wertheimer
Project Specialist: Micaela Clark
Editor: Olivia Ngai
Design & Production: Rachel Lopez Metzger

Contents

Hi kids! My name is Zooey. I'm going to teach you how to play music. Using my awesome system, you don't need to know anything fancy or technical— all you need is to know your colors, be able to follow a tune, and maybe even sing along. It's easy! Once you learn my cool color-coded system, you'll be able to play a bunch of songs you probably already recognize, just by pressing the colors on the keyboard. Let's play!

Good Piano Posture
also known as The Pro's Pose!

It may not seem important at first, but when you sit down to play, the way you sit on the bench or chair plays a part in how good your music sounds. Follow this diagram to look and sound like a pro:

1. Let your upper arms hang loose and relaxed from your shoulder.

2. Keep your back straight and lean forward slightly.

3. You want your elbows slightly higher than the keyboard to get the best sound from the keys (you may need to adjust the seat height or sit on a book to get things just right).

4. Sit on the front half of the bench or chair so that your weight is positioned forward toward the keyboard.

5. Position yourself so that your knees are slightly underneath the keyboard.

6. Keep your feet flat on the floor. If they don't touch, put some books or a step underneath them.

7. Use rounded hands to strike the keys—hold your wrists above the keyboard and arch your fingers down toward the keys.

That's it! Now you look like a rock star!

How to Use This Book

Now that you look cool at the keyboard, you're just five steps away from playing your first song! Here's how:

1 **Cut out the color-coded labels** on page 63 or 65. Be sure to set aside the red "Middle C" label, because this one is special. The letters on the labels represent the musical notes on the keyboard. So, red labels represent C notes in music; yellow labels represent E notes; blue labels represent G notes; etcetera.

> *TIP: To make the labels last longer, ask your parent or teacher to laminate the sheet of labels before cutting them.*

2 **Attach the "Middle C" label to the keyboard.** It's the one nearest the center of the keyboard that's shaped like an "L". You can use tape or removable blue putty to secure the label.

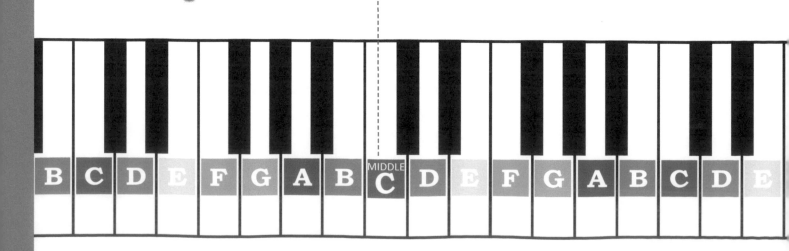

Middle **C** is the C key nearest the center of the keyboard.

3 Once you have attached the Middle C, **follow the diagram** on the top of the pages for the song you want to play to attach the rest of the color-coded labels.

> **TIP:** Put any loose labels into a covered container and tuck them into a drawer or your piano bench for storage.

The Itsy Bitsy Spider

4 Again referring to the diagram, **place your hands in the correct position** for playing the song. Then, shift your attention to the song and begin to play, pressing the keys with the colors and using the correct finger as shown.

Twinkle, Twinkle Little Star

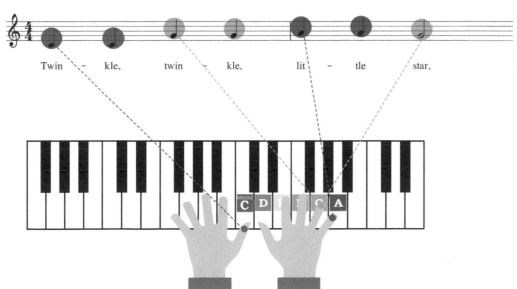

5 **Have fun!** Once you get the hang of it, you'll be able to play a ton of new songs. Look for me throughout the book—I'll be giving you extra tips and tricks so you'll become even more of a rock star as you go.

Let's Get Started!

Before you dive in and play your first song, I want to tell you about a few things you're going to see in the pages that follow.

First, you'll notice that each song is shown on a series of five horizontal lines. This set of lines is called a **staff**. You don't need to worry about this yet—your focus will be on the colors—but the music notes get placed on the staff and represent specific keys on the piano.

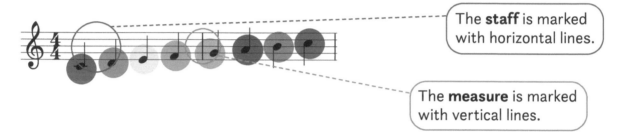

> The **staff** is marked with horizontal lines.

> The **measure** is marked with vertical lines.

Next, the staff is divided into individual sections, each separated by a vertical line. Each section between the vertical lines is called a **measure**. These measures help divide the song into smaller bits that make it easier to learn how to play.

There's also something called the **time signature**. The time signature tells you how to count the music.

 The top number tells you how many beats are in each measure. (Ignore the bottom number for now.)

For example, if you see:  there are 4 beats in the measure

 there are 3 beats in the measure

there are 2 beats in the measure

Time to Warm Up!

Professional rock stars always warm up before their gigs.
Here's a cool way for you to warm up too—the scale.

 1 Follow the diagram below to attach the color-coded labels to the keyboard.

2 Starting with your left pinkie and ending with your right pinkie, play each colored key one at a time.

3 Do the same thing again, only backwards: start with your right pinkie and play each note until you reach your left pinkie.

4 Repeat steps 2 and 3 a few times until your fingers feel nice and loose. Do this every time you sit down at the keyboard.

Now, let's try some exercises.

Exercise 1

Good to know: If you see a note that looks like

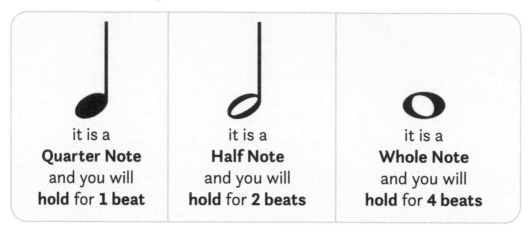

it is a **Quarter Note** and you will **hold** for **1 beat**	it is a **Half Note** and you will **hold** for **2 beats**	it is a **Whole Note** and you will **hold** for **4 beats**

Now you try: Clap out the **rhythm** and **sing.**

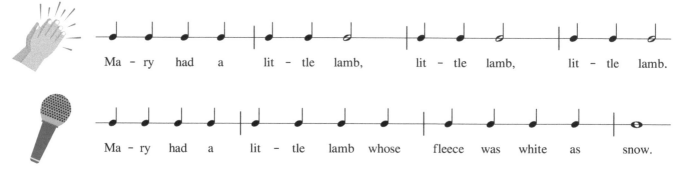

Ma – ry   had   a   lit – tle   lamb,   lit – tle   lamb,   lit – tle   lamb.

Ma – ry   had   a   lit – tle   lamb   whose   fleece   was   white   as   snow.

Start to play: Using your right hand, practice the notes you will play.

RESTING   PLAYING

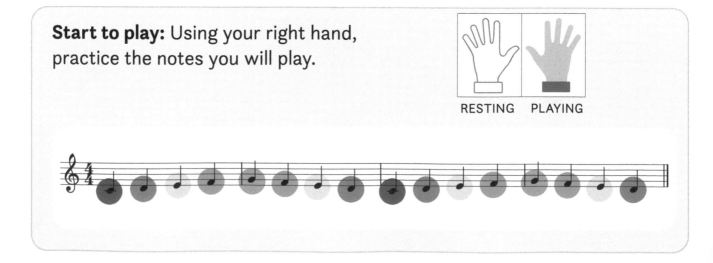

Got it? Good. Let's try playing the first song.

Twinkle, Twinkle Little Star

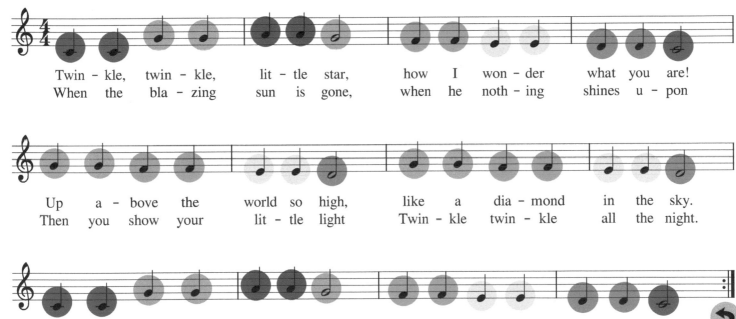

Twin – kle,   twin – kle,   lit – tle star,   how   I   won – der   what   you   are!
When   the   bla – zing   sun   is gone,   when he   noth – ing   shines u – pon

Up   a – bove   the   world so high,   like   a   dia – mond   in   the sky.
Then   you show your   lit – tle light   Twin – kle twin – kle   all   the night.

Twin – kle,   twin – kle,   lit – tle star,   how   I   won – der   what   you   are!
Twin – kle,   twin – kle,   lit – tle star,   how   I   won – der   what   you   are!

Repeat
1 time

Exercise 2

Remember: If you see a note that looks like

		NEW!	
it is a **Quarter Note** and you will **hold** for **1 beat**	it is a **Half Note** and you will **hold** for **2 beats**	it is a **Dotted Half Note** and you will **hold** for **3 beats**	it is a **Whole Note** and you will **hold** for **4 beats**

NEW! Tied notes are held down, not played again.

Hold for   1,   2,   3,   4,   5

Now you try: Clap out the **rhythm** and **sing.**

Oh   when   the   saints   go   march – ing   in   Oh   when   the

Start to play: Practice the rhythm and notes you will play. Remember to hold the piano key down for tied notes.

Play and hold the tied notes

1, 2, 3,   1, 2, 3

It – sy,   bit – sy   spi – der   went   up   the   wa – ter   spout.

The Itsy Bitsy Spider

Exercise 3

New! If you see a note that looks like

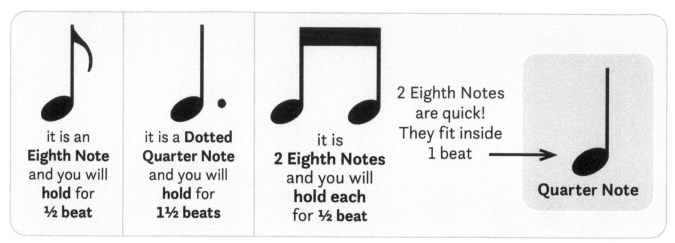

| it is an **Eighth Note** and you will **hold** for ½ beat | it is a **Dotted Quarter Note** and you will **hold** for 1½ beats | it is **2 Eighth Notes** and you will **hold each** for ½ beat | 2 Eighth Notes are quick! They fit inside 1 beat → **Quarter Note** |

Now you try: Clap out the **rhythm** and **sing**

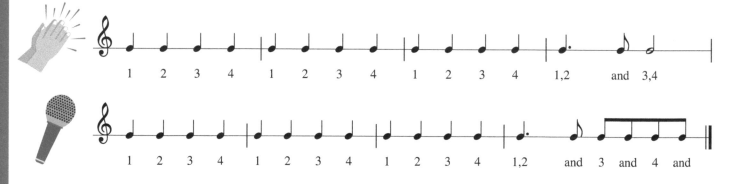

Start to play: Practice the rhythm you will play.

Got it? Good. Let's try playing some pieces.

Amazing Grace JOHN NEWTON

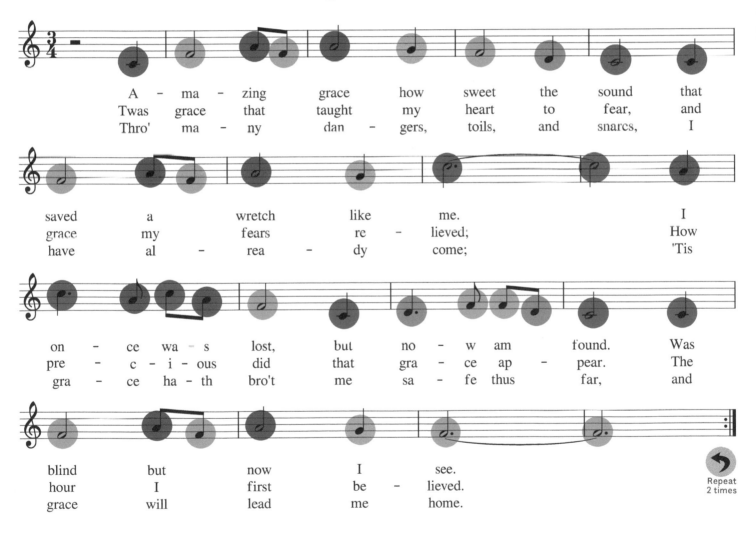

My Bonnie Lies Over the Ocean SCOTTISH FOLK SONG

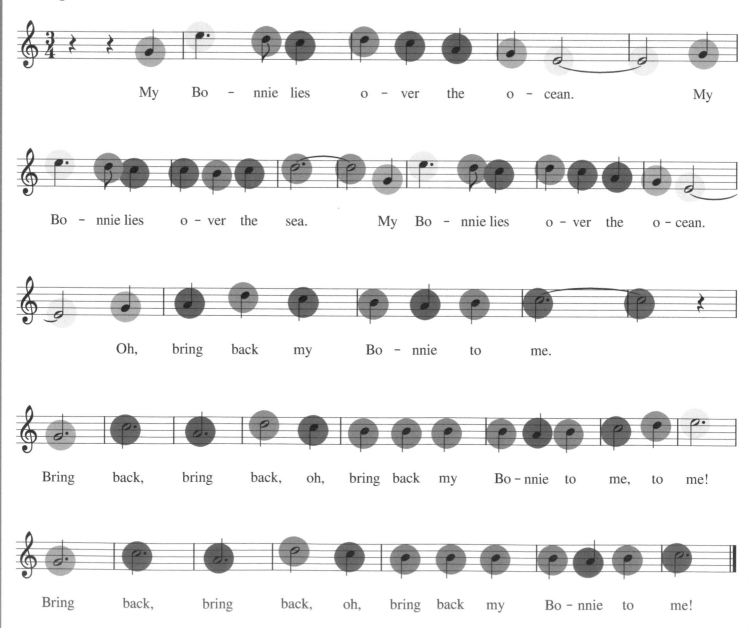

My Bo - nnie lies o - ver the o - cean. My

Bo - nnie lies o - ver the sea. My Bo - nnie lies o - ver the o - cean.

Oh, bring back my Bo - nnie to me.

Bring back, bring back, oh, bring back my Bo - nnie to me, to me!

Bring back, bring back, oh, bring back my Bo - nnie to me!

Exercise 4

Play with the correct finger:
Sometimes you will need to move your hand to reach
the keys. We number the fingers to show you how to play.

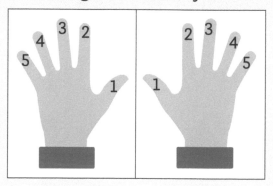

Sharps ♯ and **Flats** ♭

Have you noticed that we're only playing on the white keys? Well, the
black keys can also be played. They are called **sharps** and **flats**.

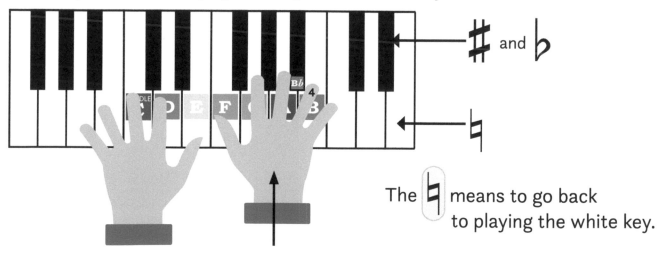

♯ and ♭

♮

The ♮ means to go back
to playing the white key.

Practice moving your hand ↑ and ↓ to go between ♭ and ♮

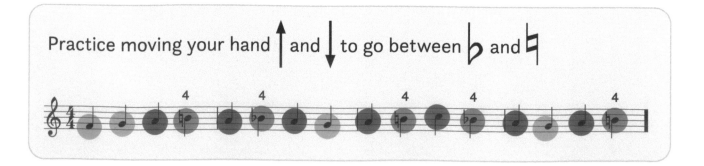

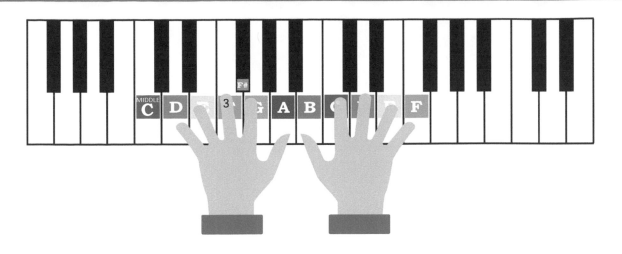

Pomp and Circumstance EDWARD ELGAR

Quarter Note Rest
for 1 beat
(turn to page 48 to
learn more!)

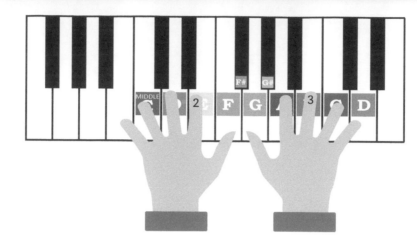

Take Me Out to the Ball Game

JACK NORWORTH,
ALBERT VON TILZER

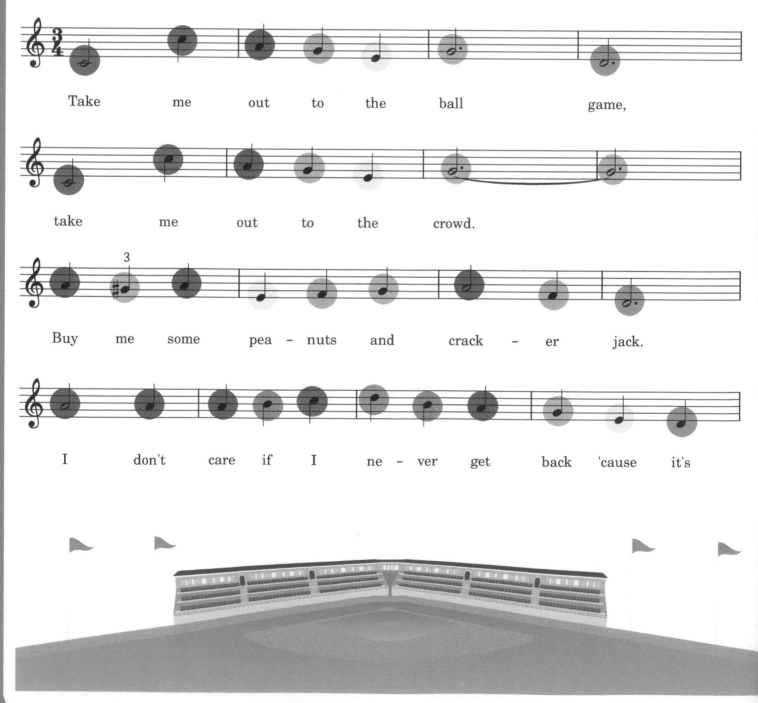

Take me out to the ball game,

take me out to the crowd.

Buy me some pea - nuts and crack - er jack.

I don't care if I ne - ver get back 'cause it's

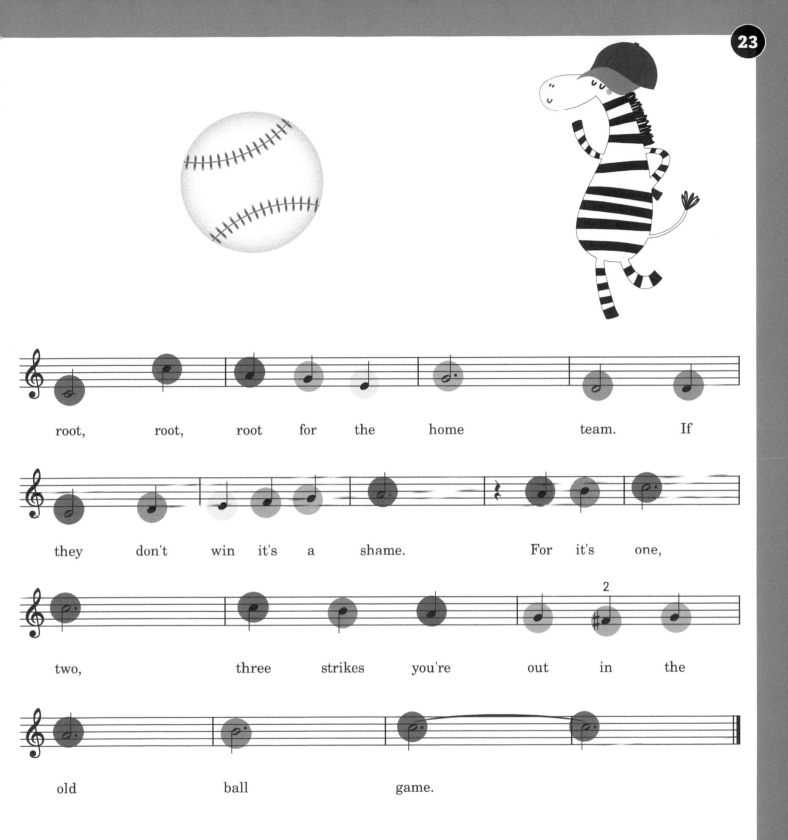

root, root, root for the home team. If

they don't win it's a shame. For it's one,

two, three strikes you're out in the

old ball game.

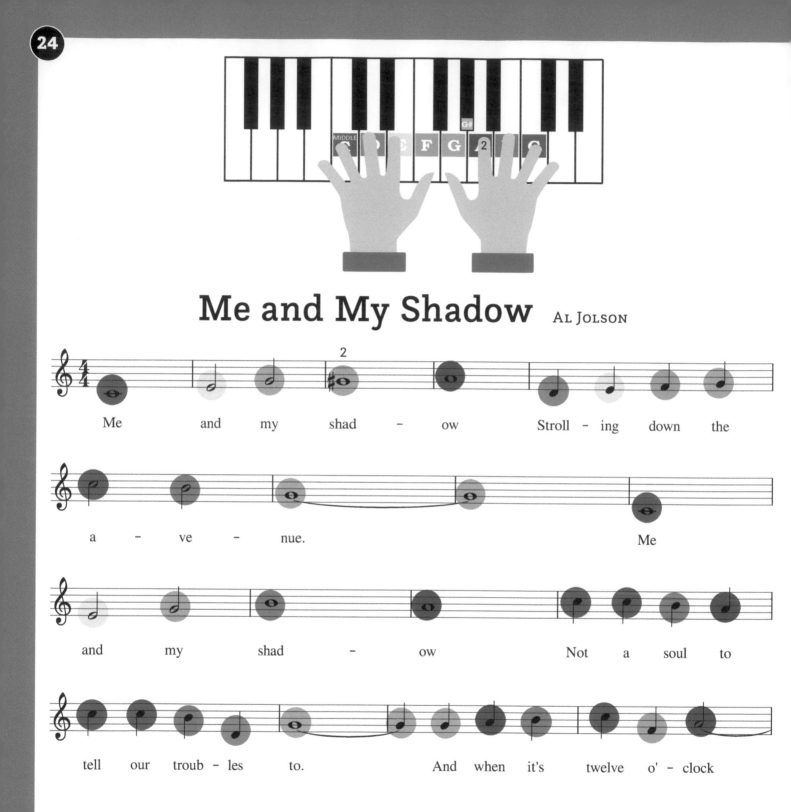

Me and My Shadow AL JOLSON

Me and my shad – ow Stroll – ing down the

a – ve – nue. Me

and my shad – ow Not a soul to

tell our troub – les to. And when it's twelve o' - clock

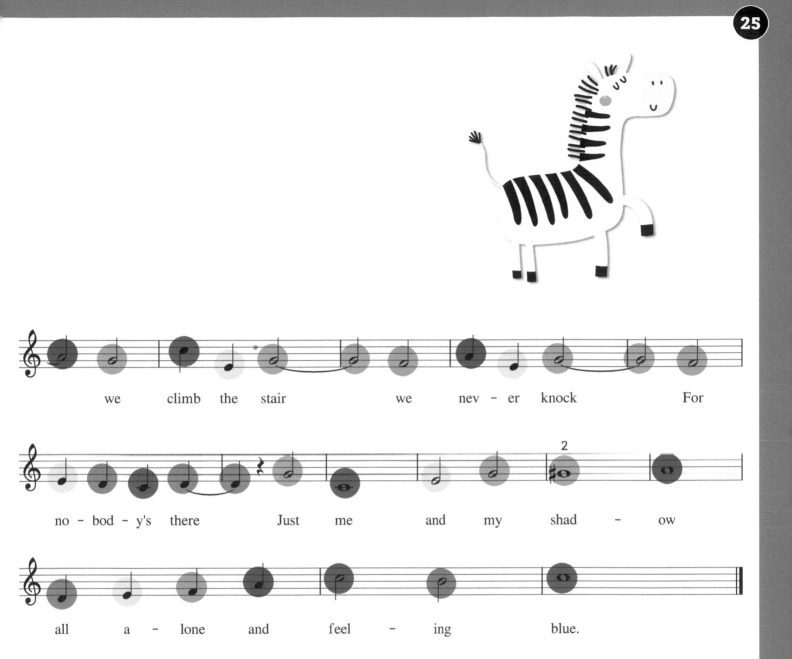

we   climb   the   stair   we   nev – er   knock   For

no – bod – y's   there   Just   me   and   my   shad –   ow

all   a – lone   and   feel – ing   blue.

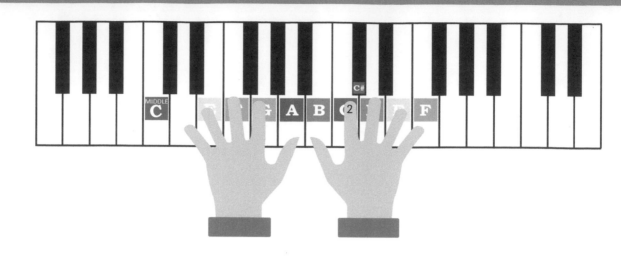

Give My Regards to Broadway   GEORGE M. COHAN

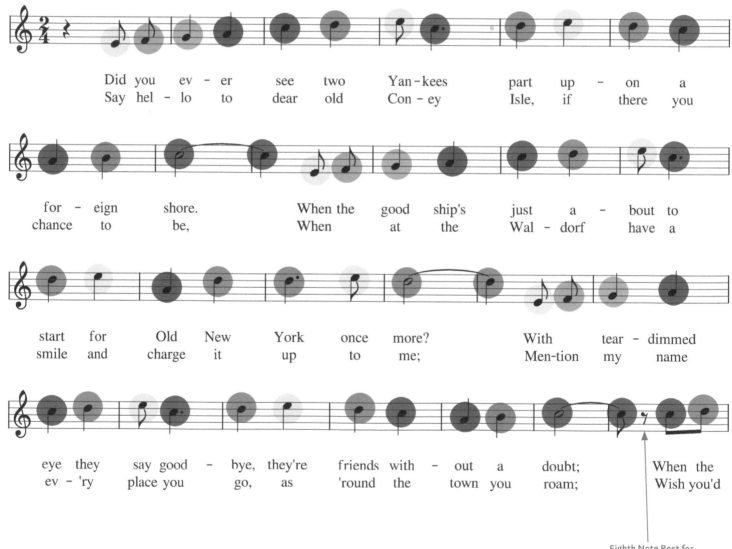

Did you ev - er see two Yan - kees part up - on a
Say hel - lo to dear old Con - ey Isle, if there you

for - eign shore. When the good ship's just a - bout to
chance to be, When at the Wal - dorf have a

start for Old New York once more? With tear - dimmed
smile and charge it up to me; Men - tion my name

eye they say good - bye, they're friends with - out a doubt; When the
ev - 'ry place you go, as 'round the town you roam; Wish you'd

Eighth Note Rest for
½ beat
(turn to page 48
to learn more!)

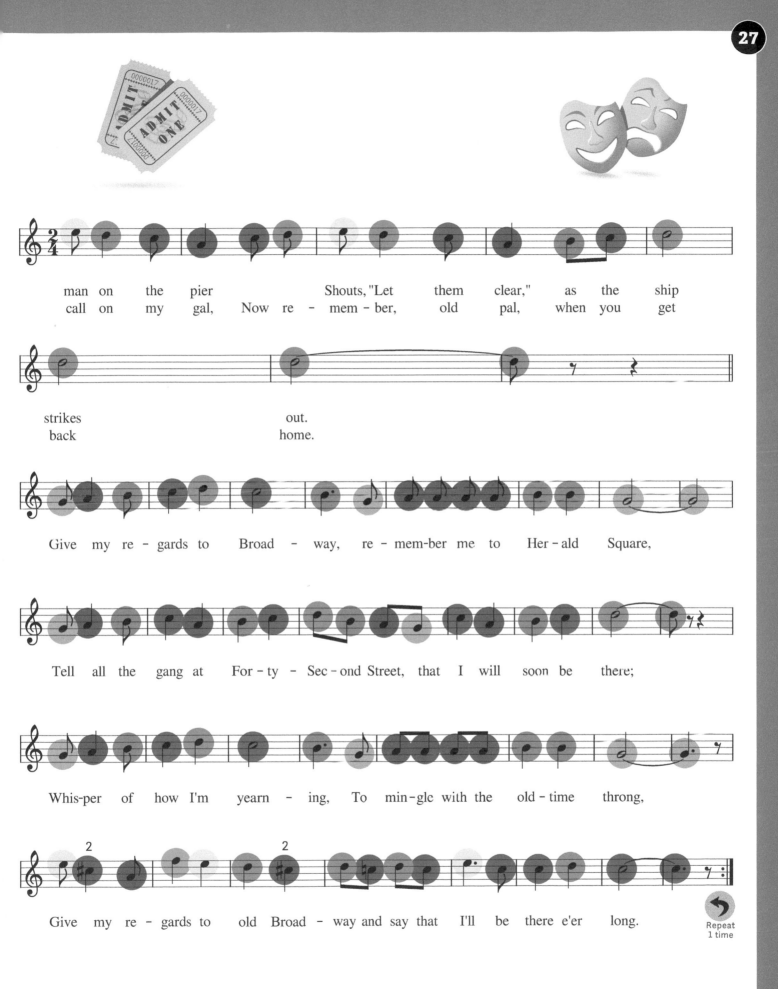

man on the pier   Shouts, "Let   them   clear,"   as the   ship
call on my gal,   Now re - mem - ber,   old   pal,   when you   get

strikes   out.
back   home.

Give my re - gards to   Broad - way,   re - mem-ber me to   Her - ald   Square,

Tell all the gang at   For - ty - Sec - ond Street,   that I will   soon be   there;

Whis-per of how I'm   yearn - ing,   To min-gle with the   old - time   throng,

Give my re - gards to   old Broad - way and say that   I'll   be   there e'er   long.

Repeat
1 time

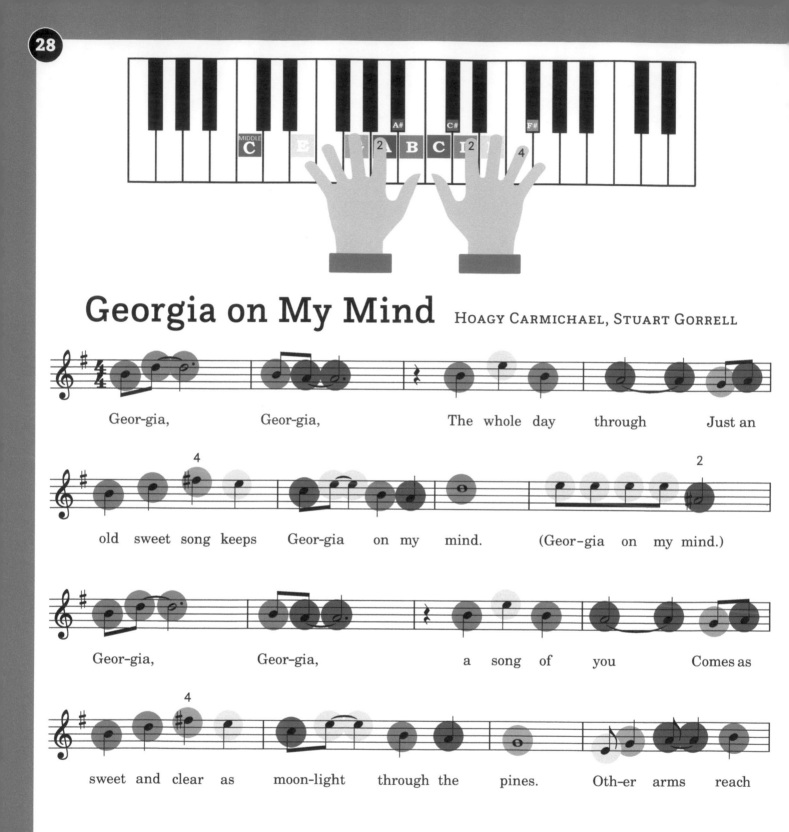

Georgia on My Mind
HOAGY CARMICHAEL, STUART GORRELL

Geor-gia,   Geor-gia,   The whole day through Just an

old sweet song keeps Geor-gia on my mind.   (Geor-gia on my mind.)

Geor-gia,   Geor-gia,   a song of you Comes as

sweet and clear as moon-light through the pines. Oth-er arms reach

Exercise 5

Remember: The notes are placed on the staff in a specific way.

The notes in the **spaces** spell

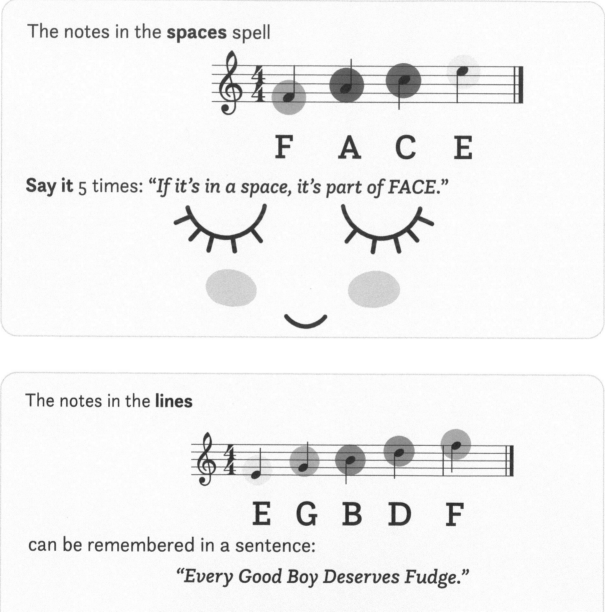

F A C E

Say it 5 times: *"If it's in a space, it's part of FACE."*

The notes in the **lines**

E G B D F

can be remembered in a sentence:

"Every Good Boy Deserves Fudge."

Say it 5 times: *"Every Good Boy Deserves Fudge."*

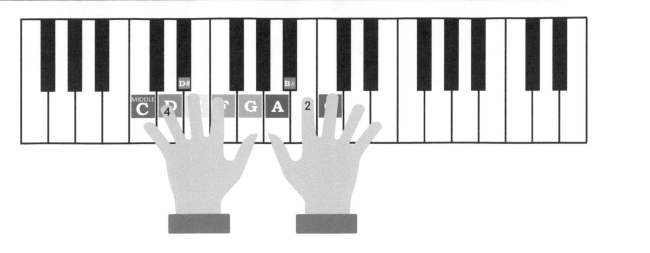

I'm Just Wild About Harry

NOBLE SISSLE, EUBIE BLAKE

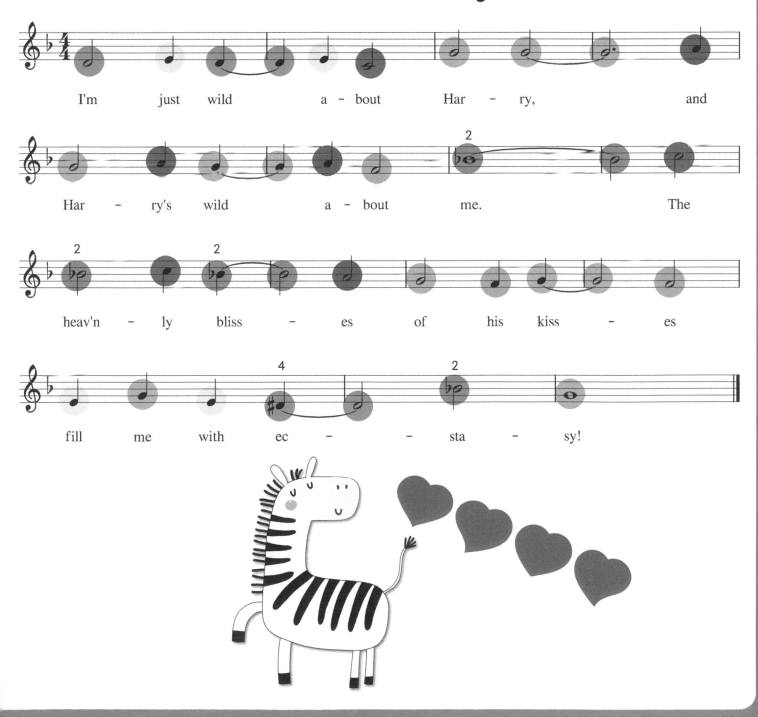

I'm   just   wild   a - bout   Har - ry,   and

Har - ry's   wild   a - bout   me.   The

heav'n - ly   bliss - es   of   his   kiss - es

fill   me   with   ec - - sta - sy!

Beautiful Dreamer STEPHEN FOSTER

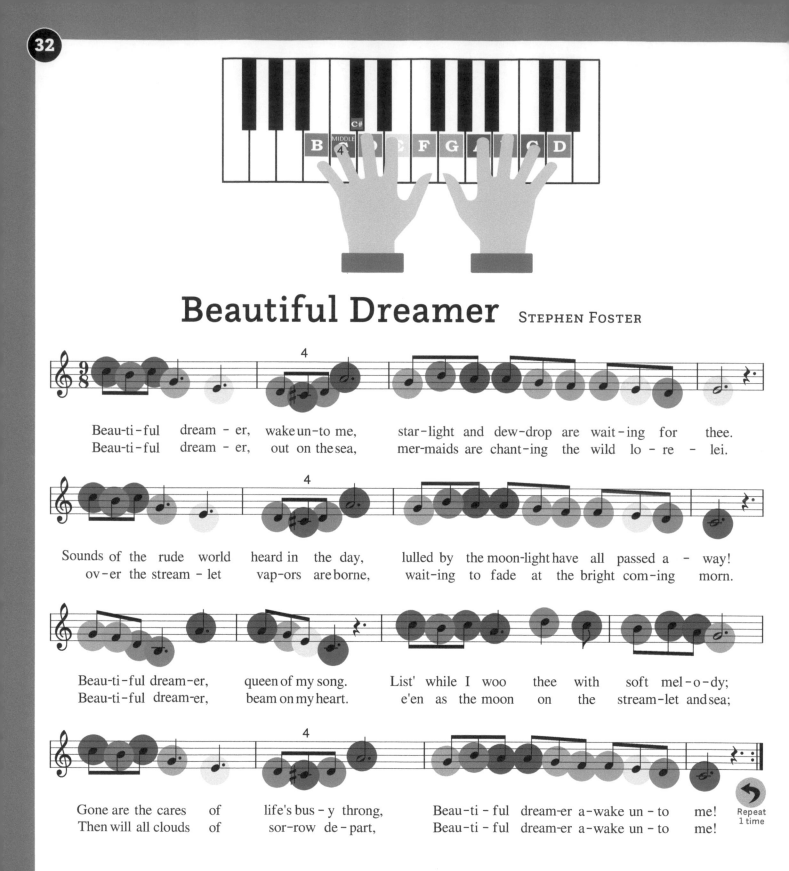

Beau-ti-ful dream - er, wake un-to me, star-light and dew-drop are wait-ing for thee.
Beau-ti-ful dream - er, out on the sea, mer-maids are chant-ing the wild lo - re - lei.

Sounds of the rude world heard in the day, lulled by the moon-light have all passed a - way!
ov-er the stream - let vap-ors are borne, wait-ing to fade at the bright com-ing morn.

Beau-ti-ful dream-er, queen of my song. List' while I woo thee with soft mel-o-dy;
Beau-ti-ful dream-er, beam on my heart. e'en as the moon on the stream-let and sea;

Gone are the cares of life's bus - y throng, Beau-ti - ful dream-er a-wake un - to me!
Then will all clouds of sor-row de - part, Beau-ti - ful dream-er a-wake un - to me!

Repeat
1 time

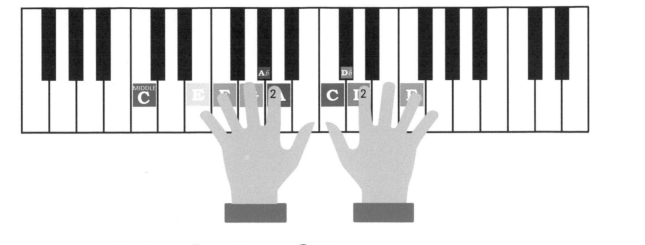

Maple Leaf Rag Scott Joplin

Yankee Doodle Boy
GEORGE M. COHAN

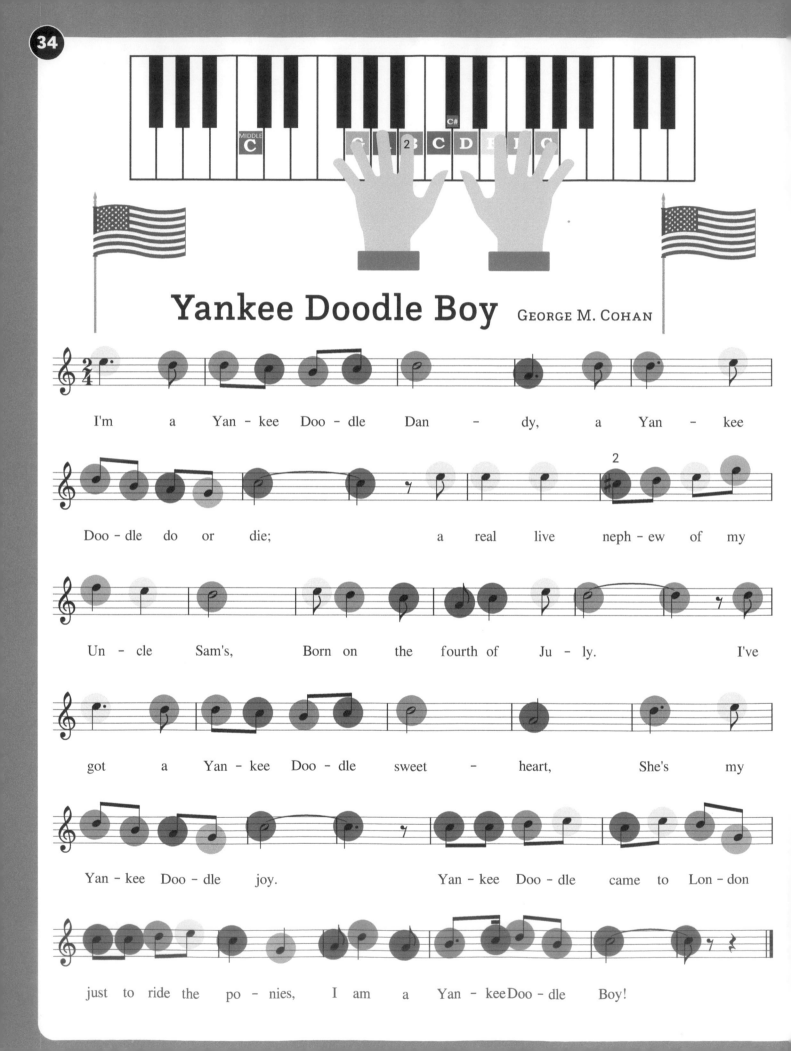

I'm a Yan - kee Doo - dle Dan - dy, a Yan - kee

Doo - dle do or die; a real live neph - ew of my

Un - cle Sam's, Born on the fourth of Ju - ly. I've

got a Yan - kee Doo - dle sweet - heart, She's my

Yan - kee Doo - dle joy. Yan - kee Doo - dle came to Lon - don

just to ride the po - nies, I am a Yan - kee Doo - dle Boy!

Quiz Time!

Don't worry, you've got this!

Name the **notes** below.

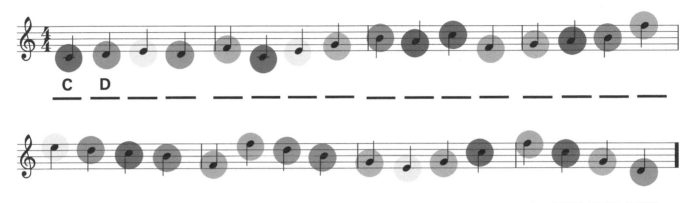

C   D

How many **beats** does each play for?

1   1

Complete the sentence:

"If it's in a space, it's part of _____"

"Every good boy _____ _____"

Exercise 6

NEW! Changing the hand positions:
Hands can move up and down the full keyboard by walking
your first three fingers up and down the keyboard.

Your thumb will go under finger 3 as you "walk" up the keyboard.
(Remember to press the black keys too!)

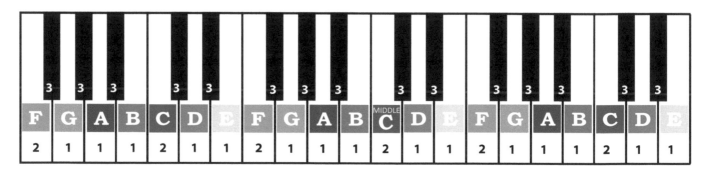

 Cross a thumb under a finger going up
(to the right)

Cross finger over thumb going down
(to the left)

Now you try: Walk your right hand up and down the keyboard by
crossing one finger over another again and again using the diagram
above. Remember to use your middle finger on the black keys!

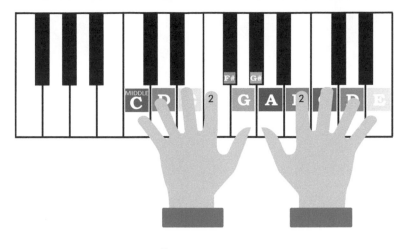

Original Rags SCOTT JOPLIN

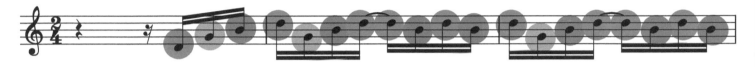

Repeat
1 time

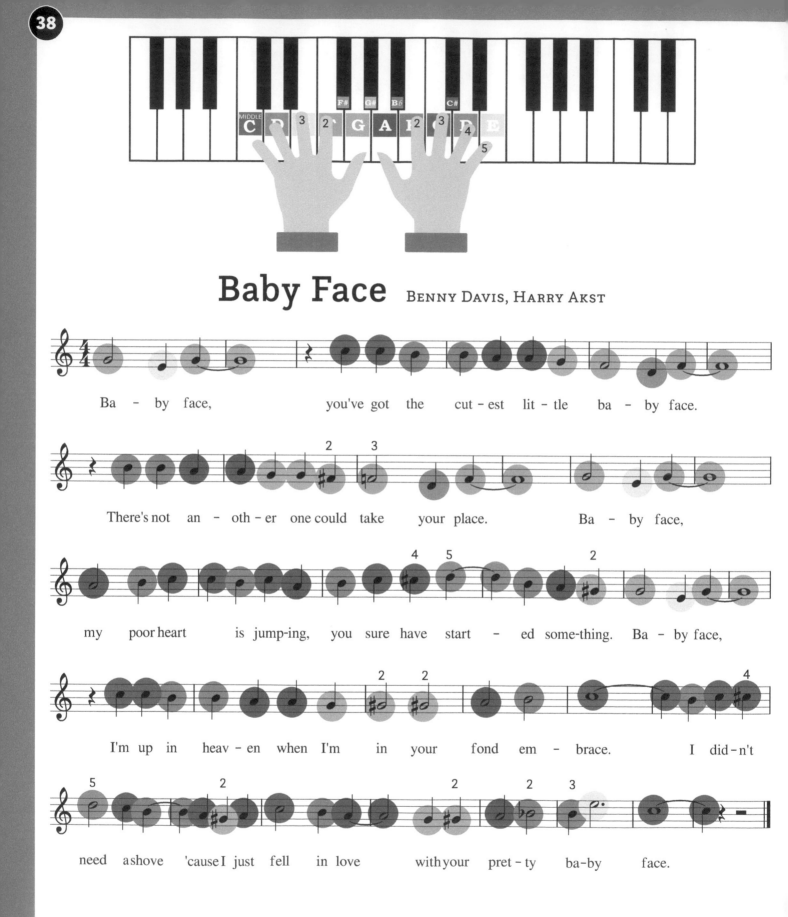

Baby Face BENNY DAVIS, HARRY AKST

Ba - by face, you've got the cut - est lit - tle ba - by face.

There's not an - oth - er one could take your place. Ba - by face,

my poor heart is jump-ing, you sure have start - ed some-thing. Ba - by face,

I'm up in heav - en when I'm in your fond em - brace. I did - n't

need a shove 'cause I just fell in love with your pret - ty ba-by face.

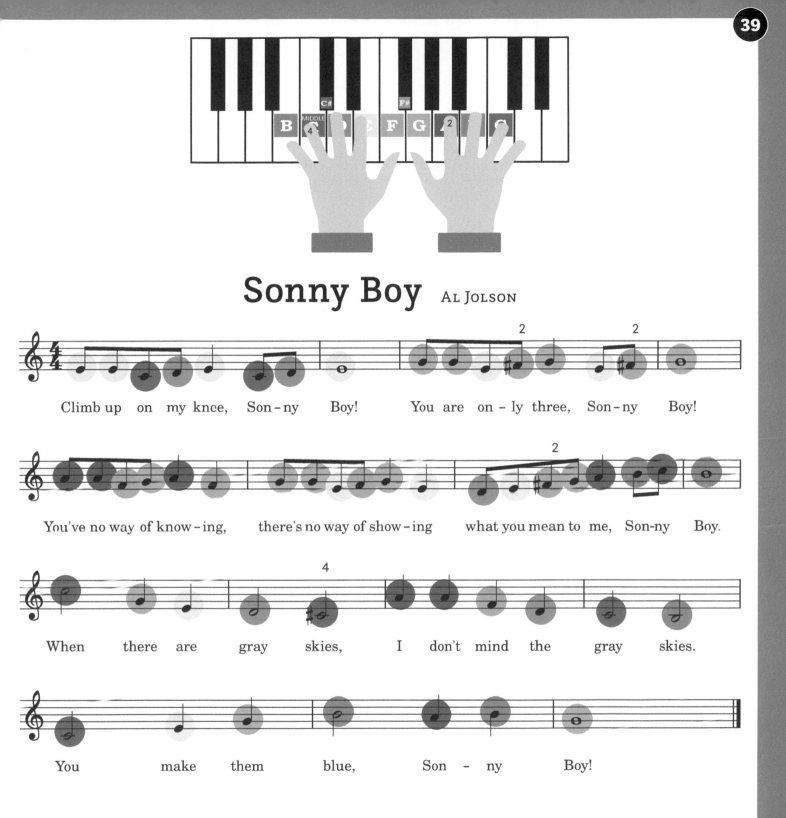

Sonny Boy AL JOLSON

Climb up on my knee, Son-ny Boy! You are on-ly three, Son-ny Boy!

You've no way of know-ing, there's no way of show-ing what you mean to me, Son-ny Boy.

When there are gray skies, I don't mind the gray skies.

You make them blue, Son-ny Boy!

California, Here I Come
AL JOLSON

Cal - i - for - nia, here I come, right back where I start - ed from.

Where bow - ers of flow - ers bloom in the sun, Each morn - ing at dawn - ing,

bird - ies sing and ev - 'ry - thing. A sun - kist miss said, "Don't be late,"

that's why I can hard - ly wait. Op - en up that

Gol - den Gate, Cal - i - for - nia, here I come.

Charleston CECIL MACK

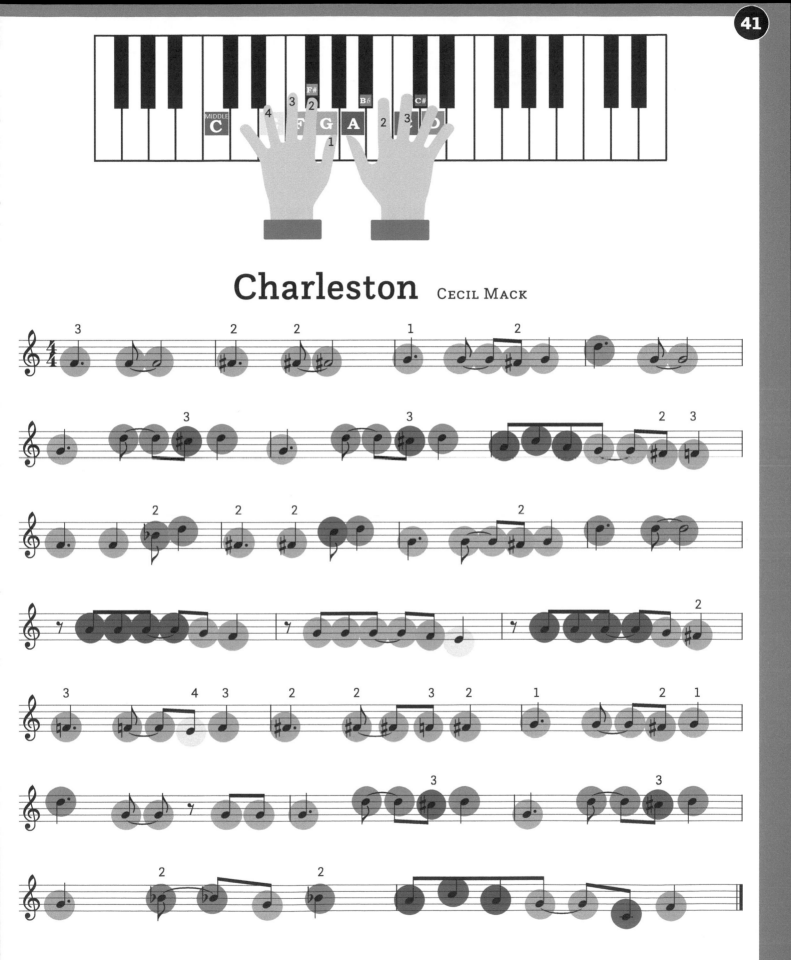

Exercise 7

NEW! Naming the hand positions: Hand position is named for the key the thumb is on.

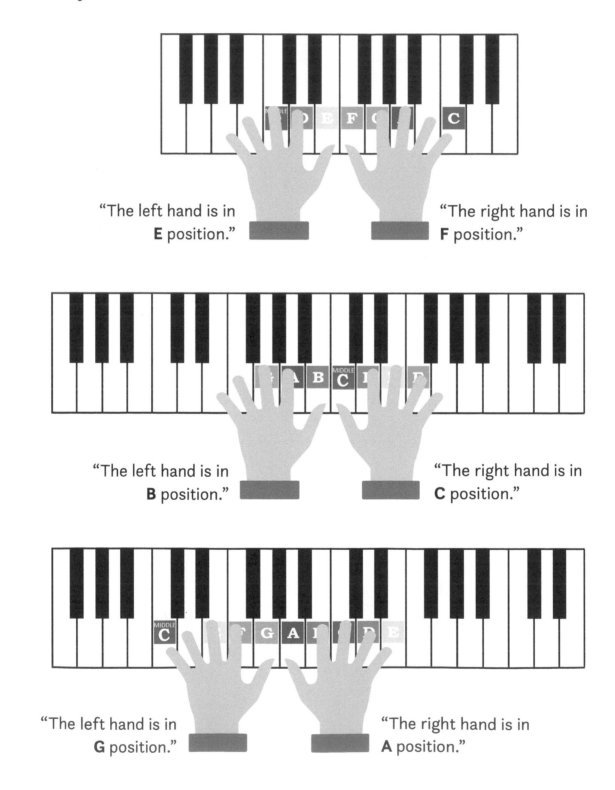

"The left hand is in **E** position."

"The right hand is in **F** position."

"The left hand is in **B** position."

"The right hand is in **C** position."

"The left hand is in **G** position."

"The right hand is in **A** position."

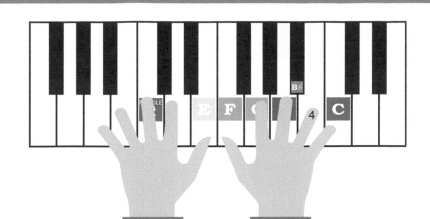

Oh My Darling, Clementine

PERCY MONTROSE

In a ca - vern, in a can - yon ex - ca - va - ting for a mine Dwelt a
Yes I loved her, how I loved her though her shoes were num-ber nine Her-ring
Drove the horse - s to the wa - ter e - very morn - ing just at nine Hit her
Ru - by lips a - bove the wa - ter blow-ing bub - bles soft and fine But a -

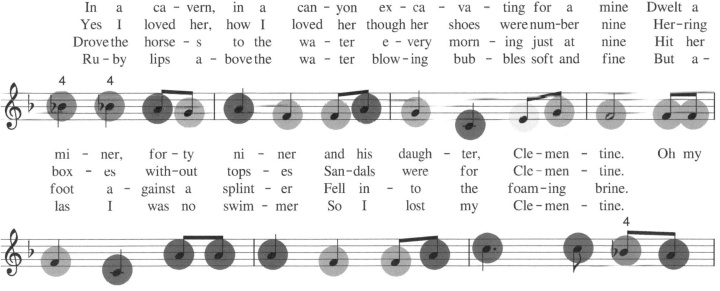

mi - ner, for - ty ni - ner and his daugh - ter, Cle - men - tine. Oh my
box - es with-out tops - es San-dals were for Cle - men - tine.
foot a - gainst a splint - er Fell in - to the foam-ing brine.
las I was no swim - mer So I lost my Cle - men - tine.

dar - ling, oh my dar - ling, oh my dar - ling, Cle - men -

tine, you are lost and gone for - ev - er. Dread-ful so - rrow, Cle-men - tine.

Repeat
3 times

April Showers LOUIS SILVERS, B. G. DE SYLVA

Though A - pril show — ers may come your way, they bring the flow - ers

that bloom in May. So if it's rain - ing, have no re - grets. Be - cause it

is - n't rain-ing rain you know, it's rain-ing vi - o - lets. And when you see clouds up-on the

hills, you soon will see crowds of daf - fo - dils. So keep on look-ing for a

blue bird, and list'ning for his song, when - ev - er A-pril show-ers come a - long.

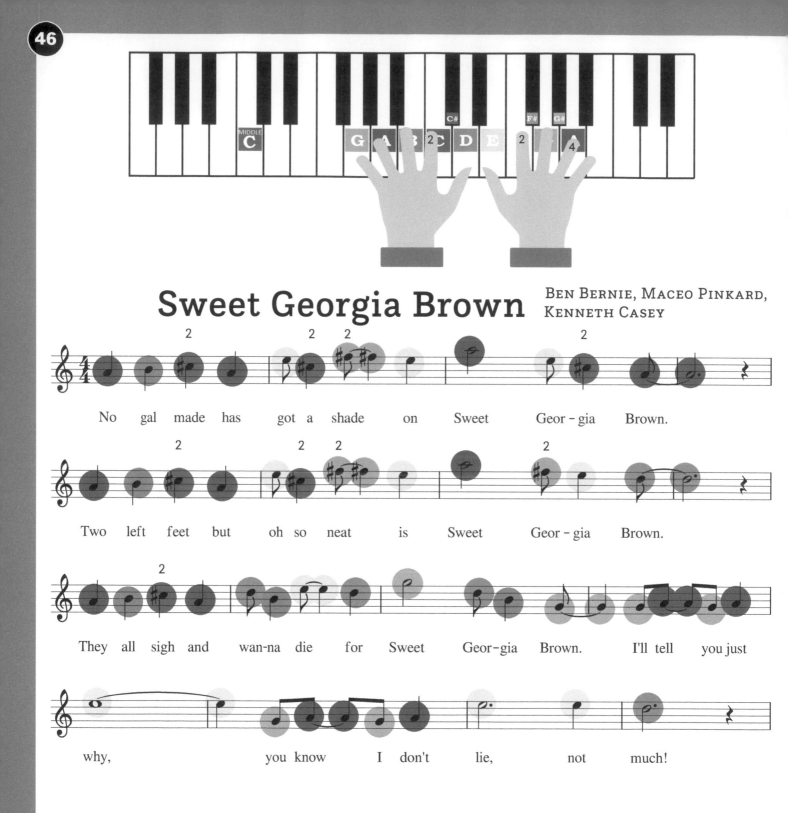

Sweet Georgia Brown

Ben Bernie, Maceo Pinkard,
Kenneth Casey

No gal made has got a shade on Sweet Geor-gia Brown.

Two left feet but oh so neat is Sweet Geor-gia Brown.

They all sigh and wan-na die for Sweet Geor-gia Brown. I'll tell you just

why, you know I don't lie, not much!

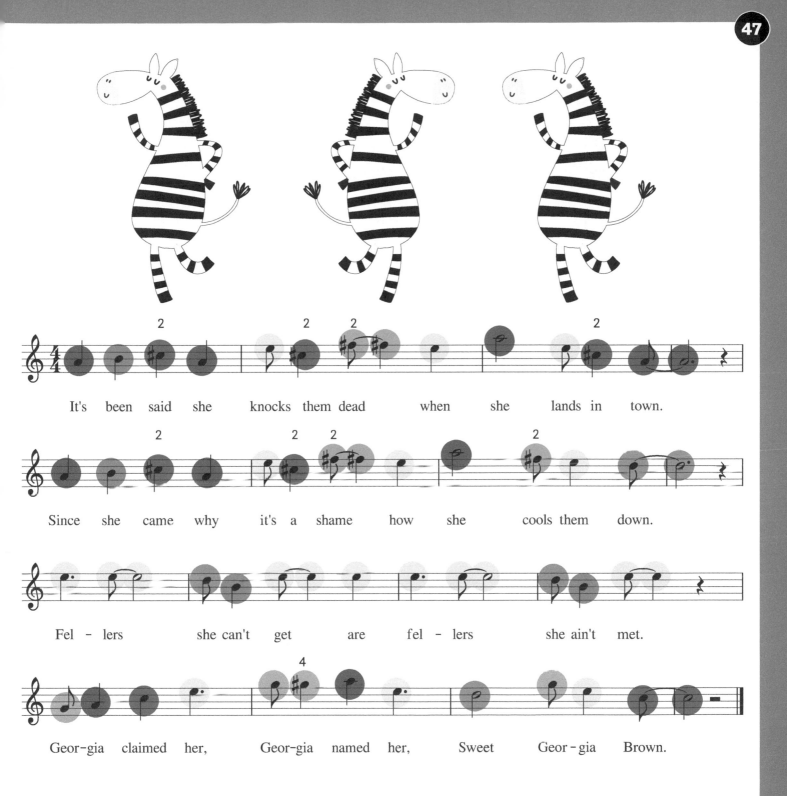

It's been said she knocks them dead when she lands in town.

Since she came why it's a shame how she cools them down.

Fel - lers she can't get are fel - lers she ain't met.

Geor-gia claimed her, Geor-gia named her, Sweet Geor - gia Brown.

Exercise 8

Remember: If you see a note that looks like

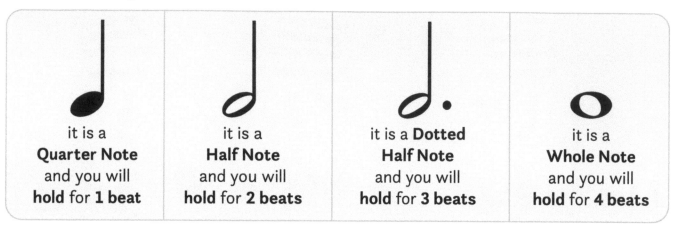

| it is a **Quarter Note** and you will **hold** for **1 beat** | it is a **Half Note** and you will **hold** for **2 beats** | it is a **Dotted Half Note** and you will **hold** for **3 beats** | it is a **Whole Note** and you will **hold** for **4 beats** |

NEW! If you see a symbol that look like

| it is an **Eighth Note Rest** and you will **rest** for **½ beat** | it is a **Quarter Note Rest** and you will **rest** for **1 beat** | it is a **Half Note Rest** and you will **rest** for **2 beats** | you will **rest** for **3 beats** | it is a **Whole Note Rest** and you will **rest** for **4 beats** |

For every song that follows, start with the following **warm-up:**

Clap out the **rhythm** and **sing,**

then practice the **notes** you will play on each hand.

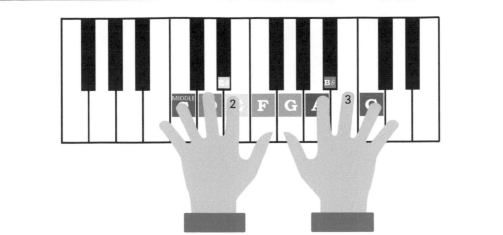

Rockin' Robin LEON RENÉ

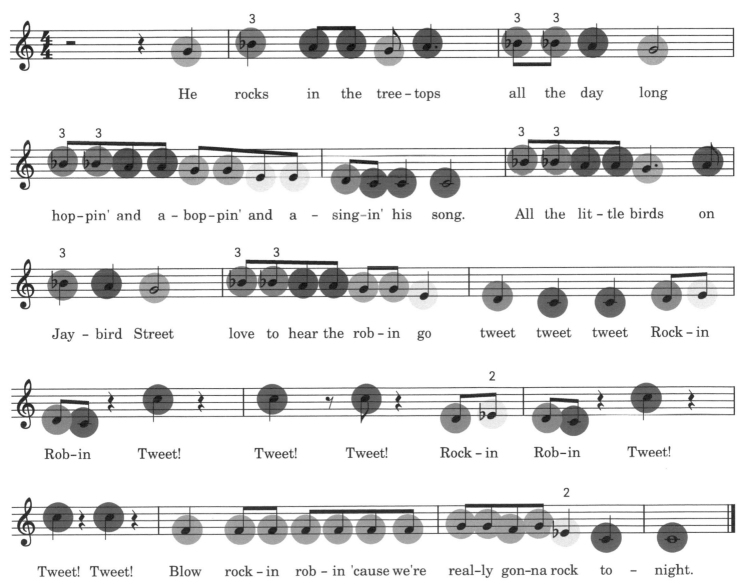

He rocks in the tree - tops all the day long

hop-pin' and a - bop-pin' and a - sing-in' his song. All the lit - tle birds on

Jay - bird Street love to hear the rob - in go tweet tweet tweet Rock - in

Rob-in Tweet! Tweet! Tweet! Rock - in Rob - in Tweet!

Tweet! Tweet! Blow rock - in rob - in 'cause we're real-ly gon-na rock to - night.

Rock of Ages THOMAS HASTINGS

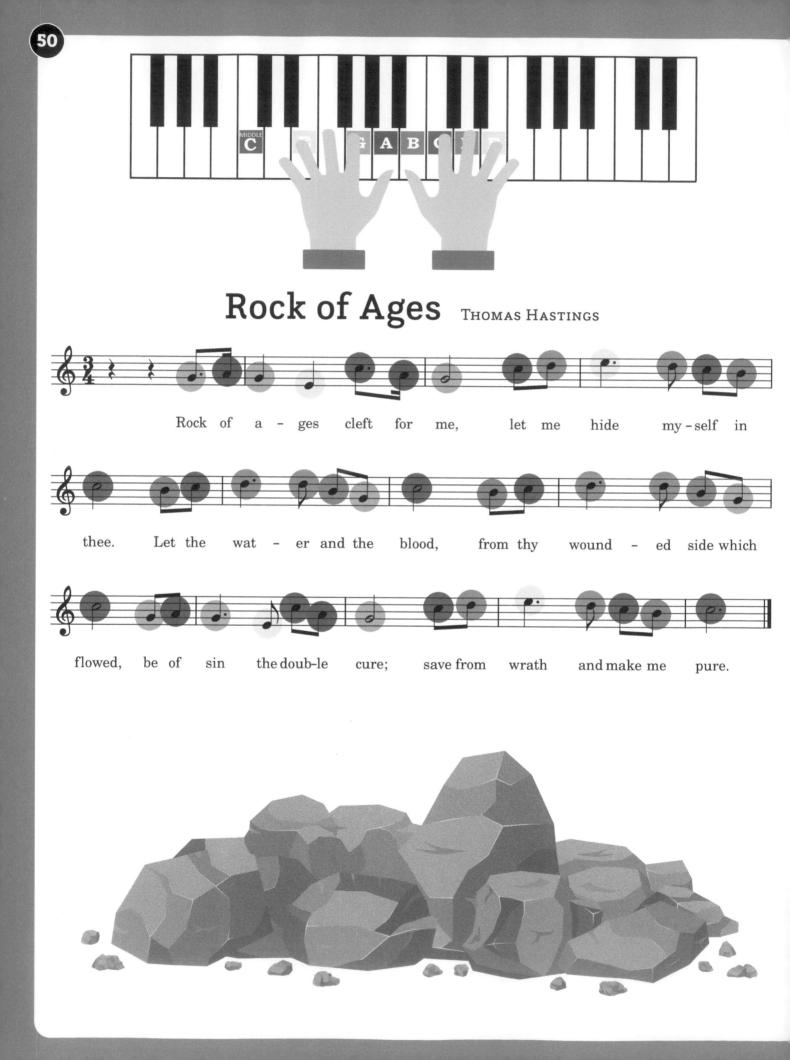

Rock of a - ges cleft for me, let me hide my - self in thee. Let the wat - er and the blood, from thy wound - ed side which flowed, be of sin the doub-le cure; save from wrath and make me pure.

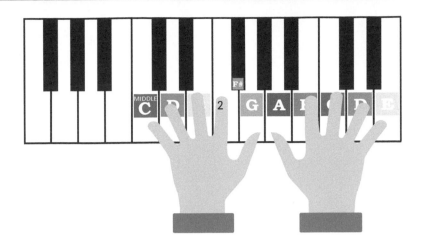

All Through the Night

WELSH FOLK SONG,
TRANSLATED BY HAROLD BOULTON

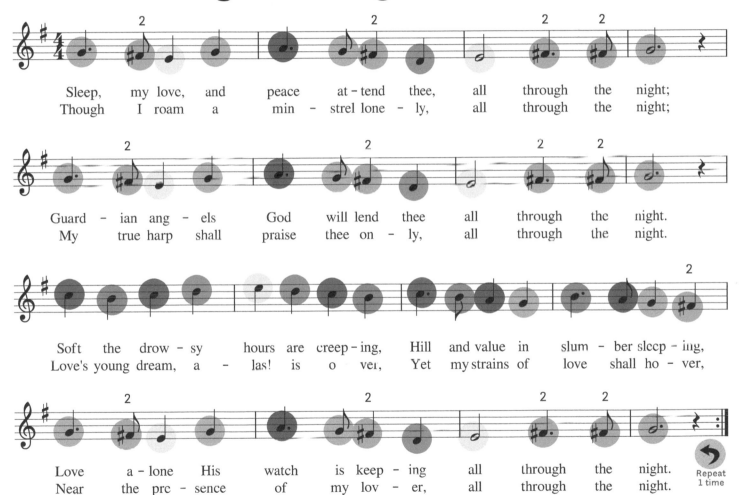

Sleep, my love, and peace at - tend thee, all through the night;
Though I roam a min - strel lone - ly, all through the night;

Guard - ian ang - els God will lend thee all through the night.
My true harp shall praise thee on - ly, all through the night.

Soft the drow - sy hours are creep - ing, Hill and value in slum - ber sleep - ing,
Love's young dream, a - las! is o - ver, Yet my strains of love shall ho - ver,

Love a - lone His watch is keep - ing all through the night.
Near the pre - sence of my lov - er, all through the night.

Repeat
1 time

You are doing a great job! Keep up the good work!

Quiz Time!

Don't worry, you've got this!
Name the **hand positions** on the keyboards below.

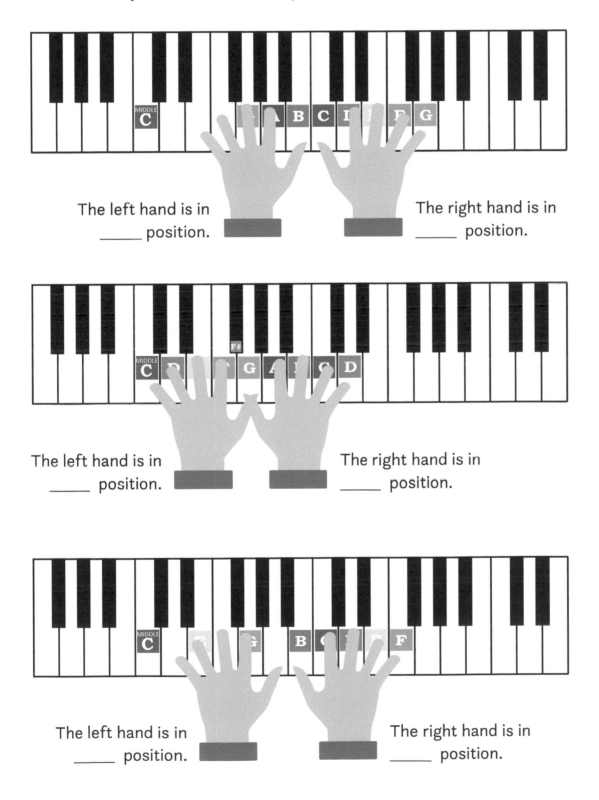

The left hand is in
_____ position.

The right hand is in
_____ position.

The left hand is in
_____ position.

The right hand is in
_____ position.

The left hand is in
_____ position.

The right hand is in
_____ position.

Someone to Watch Over Me GEORGE GERSHWIN

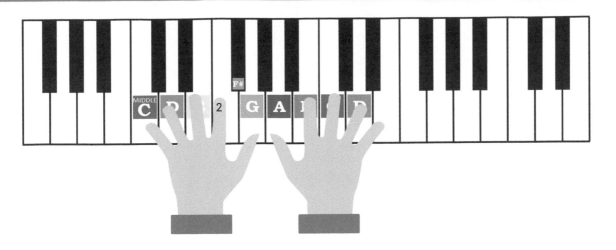

La Marseillaise CLAUDE JOSEPH ROUGET DE LISLE

Exercise 9

NEW! Changing the hand positions: **Sliding**
Sometimes you will **slide** your hands up (to the right) or
down (to the left) the keyboard to play the notes.

In the example below, the left hand moves down **three keys**: left thumb **A** to **E**.

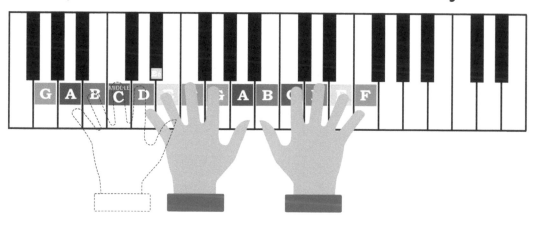

1 Move your hands together when you have to slide both hands.

2 Pay attention to the position of your thumbs, and keep them
on keys next to each other when possible.

Practice playing the final measures from the
Barber of Seville Overture on page 57.

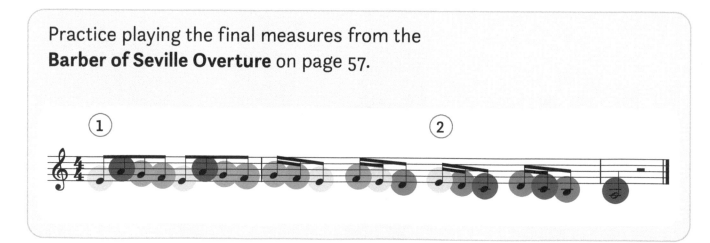

Barber of Seville Overture
GIOACHINO ROSSINI

Scarborough Fair TRADITIONAL ENGLISH BALLAD

Are you go – ing to Scar – bor – ough Fair?

Pars – ley, sage, rose – mar – y and thyme

Re – mem – ber me to one who lives there

For once she was a true love of mine.

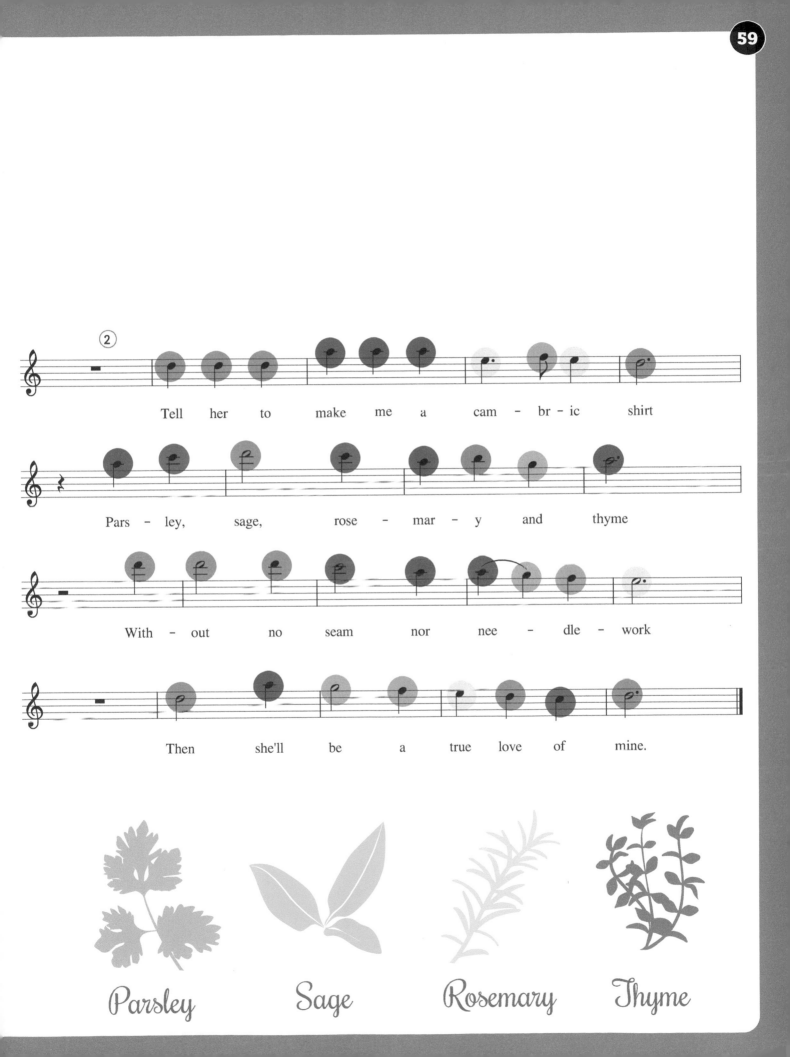

② Tell her to make me a cam - br - ic shirt

Pars - ley, sage, rose - mar - y and thyme

With - out no seam nor nee - dle - work

Then she'll be a true love of mine.

Parsley   Sage   Rosemary   Thyme

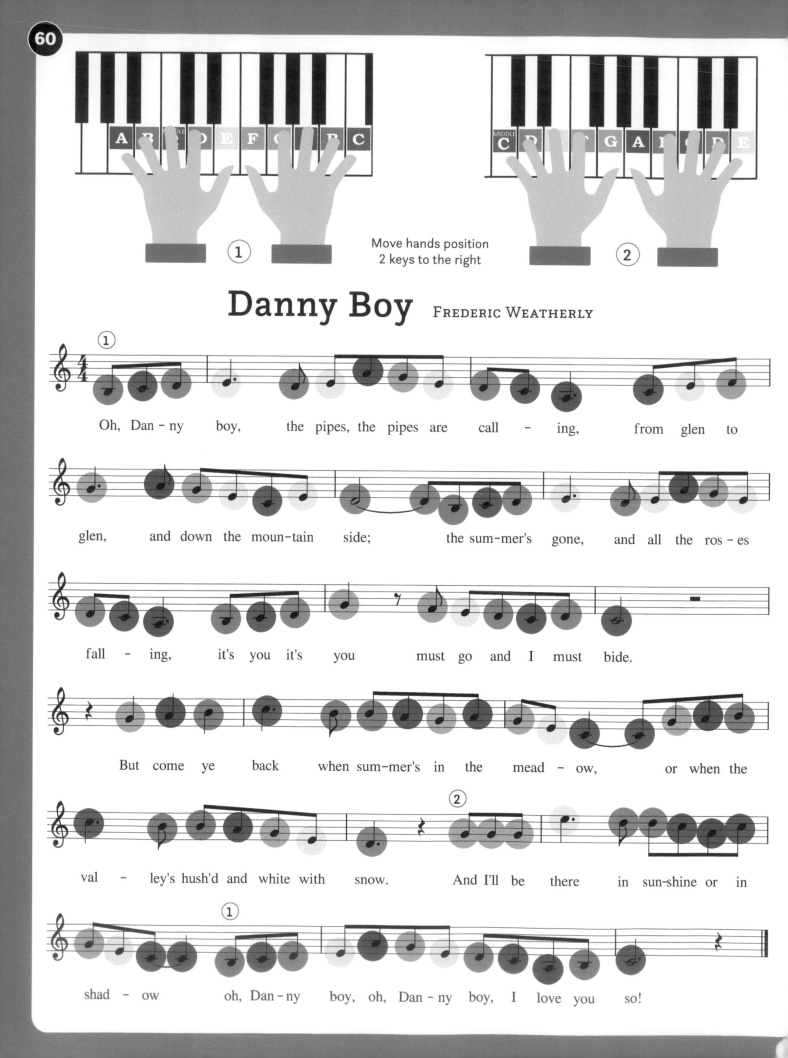

Move hands position
2 keys to the right

Danny Boy FREDERIC WEATHERLY

Oh, Dan - ny boy, the pipes, the pipes are call - ing, from glen to

glen, and down the moun-tain side; the sum-mer's gone, and all the ros - es

fall - ing, it's you it's you must go and I must bide.

But come ye back when sum-mer's in the mead - ow, or when the

val - ley's hush'd and white with snow. And I'll be there in sun-shine or in

shad - ow oh, Dan - ny boy, oh, Dan - ny boy, I love you so!

The Entertainer SCOTT JOPLIN

Lavender's Blue ENGLISH FOLK SONG

Cut the labels below and attach them to your piano keys as shown on page 8.

Standard size piano key labels

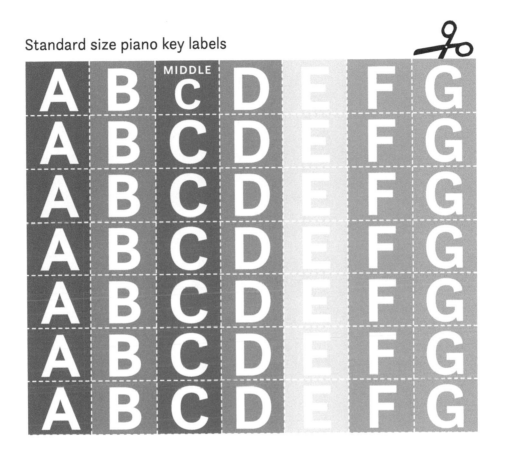

Mini key labels

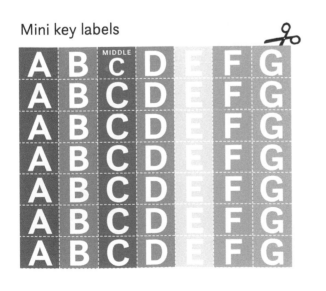

Mid-size piano key labels

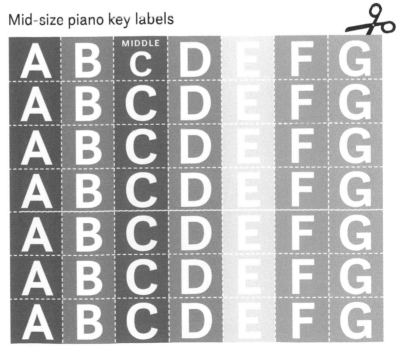

Cut the labels below and attach them to your piano keys as shown on page 8.

Standard size piano key labels

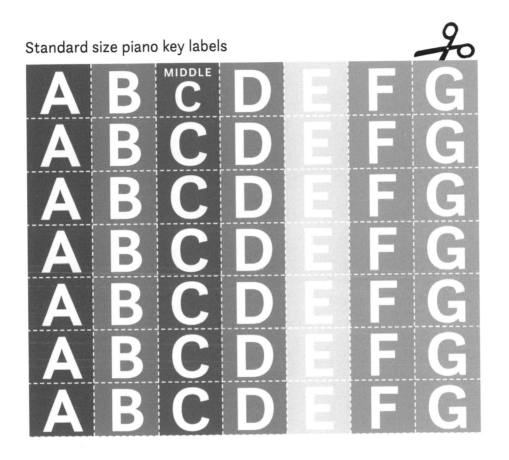

Mid-size piano key labels

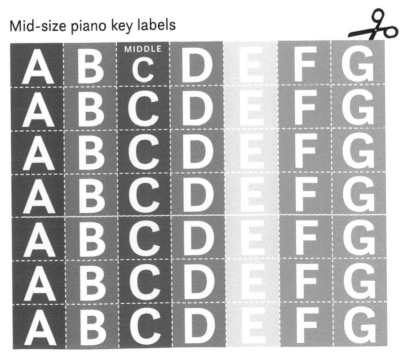

Mini key labels

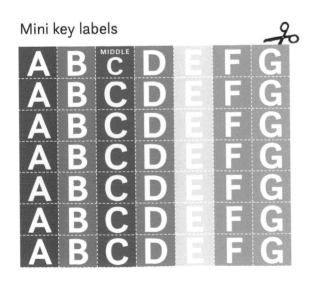

Make sure your
Play It!
library is complete